If found, please return to:

_____

_____

_____

_____

_____

Copyright

Table of Contents

Thank You!

How to Use this Book

This book is designed in my personal logical order of how to work with a novel idea. That, however, doesn't mean you must work with yours in the order this book provides. Fill the book in whichever order you want. It is meant to help you plan, not stifle your creativity.

The book starts off with a self-publishing checklist with boxes you can tick off as you go along your writing journey. Don't be discouraged by the title, though. If you want to go down the traditionally published route, there are still things in the checklist you may want to consider.

Then, the book goes into the pre-planning, outlining, and story structure stage, which intertwine with each other. There are spaces for brainstorming ideas and questions to answer. This is meant to help you come up with ideas or develop the ones you already have, and put them into a framework of a story (the story structure). Don't stay too long by questions you have no answer to, you can always go back and answer those later. Also, don't limit yourself to or search for the one and only correct or perfect answer, there are no wrong answers here. And, if you want, you can always go back and revise your answers in a later stage.

After this, we go into the project overview, which is a two-page "cheat sheet" meant to give you a better overview of your project now that you've done all the groundwork with the brainstorming, pre-writing questions, and outlines. Fill in your ideas in the overview and be proud of what you've created so far!

I have also provided a research list for you in which you can add subjects you need to research, and tick off the boxes of those you're done with.

Lastly, there is the ultimate story checklist to help you evaluate your story when you've **already written your first draft**. That way, you can use the checklist to its full potential. In other words, don't focus too much on it when you're still brainstorming ideas for your story.

Bonus tip #1: You may want to write your notes in pencil for easy erasure should your novel change with time.

"You can't use up creativity. The more you use, the more you have."

— Maya Angelou

Want to sketch something?

THE ULTIMATE SELF-PUBLISHING CHECKLIST

Cheat Sheet

Title of project: _____

Target release date: _____

Type: Ebook   Paperback   Hardcover

Length: Novel   Novella   Short Story

Estimated word count: _____

Costs

Structural edit: Book cover design:

_____   _____

Line edit: Domain name:

_____   _____

Proofread: Web hosting service:

_____   _____

Formatter: Website design / template:

_____   _____

Notes:

Deadline Overview

O **Release date**   Deadline: _____

O **Manuscript**   Deadline: _____

    O Write draft   Deadline: _____

    O Revise   Deadline: _____

    O Self-edit   Deadline: _____

    O Structural edit   Deadline: _____

    O Line edit   Deadline: _____

    O Proofread   Deadline: _____

O **Book design**   Deadline: _____

    O Format   Deadline: _____

    O Book cover   Deadline: _____

O **Publishing**   Deadline: _____

    O Upload files   Deadline: _____

    O Quality check   Deadline: _____

O **Promotion**   Deadline: _____

    O Blog tour   Deadline: _____

    O Social media   Deadline: _____

    O Ads   Deadline: _____

    O Launch party   Deadline: _____

O **Extras**   Deadline: _____

    O Set up an author website   Deadline: _____

    O Social media   Deadline: _____

Notes:

Manuscript

- O **Pre-Writing**
  - O Brainstorm ideas
  - O Pre-write questions
  - O Outline
    - O Setting
    - O Scene
    - O Character sketches
  - O Story Structure

- O **First draft**
  - O Write first draft
  - O Let it rest, how long is up to you

- O **Revision / Rewrite**
  - O The Ultimate Story Checklist
    - O Characters
    - O Setting
    - O Plot
    - O Point-of-view
    - O Dialogue
  - O Name consistency (character names, place / setting names, organizations, etc.)
  - O Fix poor sentences
  - O Fix poor grammar
- O **Professional edit**
- O **Structural edit**

- O Hire editor
  - O Research who fits your needs and budget
  - O Contact Editor
    - O Request sample, if possible
    - O Word / page count
    - O Genre
    - O Summary
    - O Deadline
  - O Send payment
  - O Evaluate and implement changes
- O **Line edit**
  - O Hire editor
    - O Research who fits your needs and budget
    - O Contact Editor
      - O Request sample, if possible
      - O Word / page count
      - O Genre
      - O Summary
      - O Deadline
    - O Send payment
    - O Evaluate and implement changes
- O **Proofread**

O Hire editor
- O Research who fits your needs and budget
- O Contact Editor
  - O Request sample, if possible
  - O Word / page count
  - O Genre
  - O Summary
  - O Deadline
- O Sent payment
- O Evaluate and implement changes

Additional notes:

_____

_____

_____

_____

_____

_____

_____

_____

_____

_____

_____

_____

_____

_____

_____

_____

_____

_____

_____

_____

_____

_____

_____

_____

_____

_____

_____

_____

_____

Book Design

- **Front and back matter**
  - Front matter
    - Title page
    - Copyright page
    - Table of content (opt.)
    - Call to action / opt-in
  - Back matter
    - Call to action / opt-in
    - Also written by the author (opt.)
    - Thank you page with a request for a rate / review
    - About the Author

- **Format**
- **Hire formatter**
  - Research who fits your needs and budget
  - Contact formatter
    - Request sample, if possible
    - Word count / page count
    - Genre
    - Deadline
    - Send payment
    - Send file

- **DIY**
  - Fix font
  - Fix spacing and indents
  - Fix chapter headings
  - Insert page breaks after chapters
  - Insert images, if relevant
  - Compile to ePub (for ebooks)
  - Compile to MOBI (for ebooks)
  - Change margins and page size (for printed books)
  - Add page number (for printed books)
  - Move content / chapter starts to right-hand pages as needed, if relevant (for printed books)

- **Cover design**
- **Hire Designer**
  - Research who fits your needs and budget
  - Contact designer
    - Cover size / dimensions
      - Ebook or Paperback
    - Synopsis
    - Genre
    - Deadline

- O Send payment
- O Provide feedback

- O **DIY**
  - O Brainstorm ideas
    - O Research covers in your genre for inspiration and market research
  - O Find / purchase legal image(s)
  - O Cover size / dimensions
  - O Design the cover
    - O Add image(s)
    - O Add title and author name
    - O Add book description at the back of the cover (for printed books)
  - O Save ebook cover as JPG file
  - O Save print book cover as PDF

Additional notes:

_____

_____

_____

_____

_____

_____

_____

_____

Publishing

- ○ **Upload files**
  - ○ Create accounts on KDP and / or other sites for ebooks
  - ○ Create an account on sites for print books
    - ○ Tax information
    - ○ Royalty payment info
  - ○ Set up a new title (do this on each site)
    - ○ Title
    - ○ Series
    - ○ Author name
    - ○ Synopsis
    - ○ Categories (genre)
    - ○ Keywords
    - ○ Age range, if relevant
    - ○ ISBN (not necessary on Amazon for ebooks)
    - ○ Publishing rights (public domain or not)
    - ○ Pre-order, if relevant
    - ○ Price
  - ○ Upload JPG book cover for ebook on the chosen site(s)
  - ○ Upload ebook file on the chosen site(s)
  - ○ Upload PDF book cover and book file for printed book on the chosen site(s)

- ○ **Proof**
  - ○ Preview ebook using your own eReader
  - ○ Preview ebook using Kindle Previewer
    - ○ Check formatting consistency (table of content, indents, page breaks, placement of chapter headings, etc.)
    - ○ Check image placement, if relevant
  - ○ Order printed proof of paperback
    - ○ Check cover quality (don't forget the back of the book)
    - ○ Check the consistency of the chapter beginnings (if they all begin on the right-hand-side), if relevant

O Check formatting consistency (table of content, indents, fonts, margins, page breaks, placement of chapter headings, etc.)

O Check image placement, if relevant

O Check page numbers

O Check other errors

Additional notes:

_____

_____

_____

_____

_____

_____

_____

_____

_____

_____

_____

_____

_____

_____

Promotion

○ **Plan release**
- ○ Research the best time to release a book in the chosen genre
- ○ Set the release date
  - ○ Pre-order?
- ○ Set up a Street Team, if relevant
- ○ Prep Beta Readers to rate and leave reviews (on sites like Goodreads, Amazon, and similar), if relevant
- ○ Send out ARCs (Advanced Reader Copies), if relevant
- ○ Reach out to Amazon top reviewers
- ○ Create a Media Kit, if relevant
  - ○ Get a professional author headshot
  - ○ Write an author bio
  - ○ Make a flier with book info and links to website
  - ○ Write a press release
- ○ Get SWAG (printed materials such as business cards, bookmarks, t-shirts, fliers, etc.), if relevant

○ **Plan a blog tour**
- ○ Find potential bloggers
- ○ Write a request email
  - ○ Introduce yourself
  - ○ A summary of your book
  - ○ Mention release date of the book
  - ○ Mention around which time you would want the blog post to be published
- ○ Agree on a date for the publication of the blog post
- ○ Agree on a date for when you should send the text and graphics to the blogger
- ○ Pre-write blog posts
  - ○ Write the text for the blog post
  - ○ Create graphics for the blog post
  - ○ Provide bloggers with blog post, graphics, author and book info
- ○ Network with other authors for cross-promotion options
  - ○ Focus on authors with the audience you're targeting

○ **Organize a cover reveal**

    ○ Post on your website

    ○ Post on social media

    ○ Share in email newsletter

○ **Post launch**

    ○ Host giveaways

    ○ Set up signings

        ○ Contact local bookstores

        ○ Contact local libraries

Additional notes:

Extras

- ○ **Branding**
  - ○ How you want your author branding to be perceived?
  - ○ Ideas for logo and / or header
  - ○ Color scheme
  - ○ Fonts
- ○ **Hire a designer**
  - ○ Research who fits your needs and budget
  - ○ Contact designer
    - ○ Info about the visions of your brand
    - ○ Info about logo and / or header ideas
    - ○ Info about color scheme and fonts
    - ○ Deadline
  - ○ Send payment
  - ○ Provide feedback
- ○ **DIY**
  - ○ Download font(s), if relevant
  - ○ Find / purchase legal image(s), if relevant
  - ○ Design a logo and / or header using paid software like Photoshop / Illustrator, or similar
  - ○ Design a logo and / or header using a free tool like Canva, or similar
  - ○ Design the logo with a transparent background
  - ○ Design the logo in different sizes
  - ○ Save / download images in both JPG and PNG format
- ○ **Build an email list**
  - ○ Create an account on an email marketing provider (like MailChimp, ConvertKit, AWeber, etc.)
  - ○ Set up an email list
  - ○ Write / format the welcome email
  - ○ Design graphics, like email header, if relevant
  - ○ Design a template for the email newsletter, if relevant
- ○ **Create an author website**
- ○ **Hire a designer**
  - ○ Research who fits your needs and budget

- O Purchase domain name
- O Purchase web hosting service
- O Contact designer
  - O Info on what type of website you want
  - O Content to be included
  - O Info on functions and integrations you want
  - O Brand fonts and colors, if relevant
  - O Deadline
- O Send payment
- O Send content (logo, header, headshot, about page text, contact information, etc.)
- O Send domain and web hosting info
- O Provide feedback
- O **DIY**
  - O Brainstorm ideas
  - O Purchase domain name
  - O Purchase web hosting service
  - O Install web design software (like Wordpress), if relevant
  - O Buy / select a website theme / template
    - O Design the theme / template to your wants and needs and to fit your brand

- O Add content like about page and contact page, etc.
- O Add integrations
  - O Social media share buttons
  - O Email list sign up forms that are visible

- O **Set up social media accounts**
  - O Set up a Goodreads account (recommended)
  - O Set up a Facebook author page (if desired)
  - O Set up an author Twitter account (if desired)
  - O Set up an author Instagram account (if desired)
  - O Set up a Pinterest account (if desired)
  - O Brand all social media profiles with custom profile pictures and headers

Additional notes:

_____

_____

_____

_____

_____

_____

_____

Want to sketch something?

PRE-PLANNING

Brainstorming Ideas

Brainstorming is a great way to get interesting and unexpected ideas out of your head. It doesn't have to be a big undertaking. Set a timer for 5-10 minutes and let the ideas flow.

The next few pages are designed to let you brainstorm ideas however you want. The following pages are designated to brainstorm:
- Story ideas
- Setting ideas
- Scene ideas
- Character ideas

When you're done, go back and evaluate your ideas.
- Which are most interesting and exciting to explore?
- Which can't you wait to dive further into?
- Which do you want to incorporate into your story?
- Which will fit seamlessly into the story?

Take note and focus on those ideas that interest you. Your own engagement and excitement will seep into every part of your story.

"Brainstorming is the nexus of ideas."

— Asa Don Brown

Take 10-15 minutes to brainstorm story ideas.

Take 10-15 minutes to brainstorm setting ideas.

Take 10-15 minutes to brainstorm scene ideas.

Take 10-15 minutes to brainstorm character ideas.

Notes:

Pre-Writing Questions

Book and audience

What kind of story do you want to write? In what genre?

_____

_____

_____

_____

_____

_____

_____

What do you *not* want the story to be?

_____

_____

_____

_____

_____

_____

_____

Who is your ideal audience?

_____

_____

_____

_____

_____

_____

Why will your ideal audience want to read the story?

_____

_____

_____

_____

What will they love about the story?

_____

_____

_____

_____

Characters

Who is your main character?

_____

_____

_____

_____

_____

_____

What is her goal and motivation?

_____

_____

_____

_____

_____

_____

_____

_____

Who will oppose the main character (antagonist)?

_____

_____

_____

_____

_____

_____

_____

_____

What is the antagonist's goal and motivation?

_____

_____

_____

_____

_____

_____

_____

_____

Setting

Where does your story take place? Is it a real or fictional place? In what era?

_____

_____

_____

_____

_____

_____

_____

_____

What kind of cultural setting do you want in the story?

_____

_____

_____

_____

_____

_____

What kind of social setting do you want in the story?

_____

_____

_____

_____

_____

_____

_____

What kind of mood do you want the story to have, and how does your chosen setting enhance that mood?

_____

_____

_____

_____

_____

_____

_____

Story

Name four or five big moments that will occur in the story.

_____

_____

_____

_____

_____

_____

_____

Can you think of at least two complications for each of these moments? Will these complications make the characters uncomfortable?

_____

_____

_____

_____

_____

_____

_____

_____

_____

_____

_____

_____

_____

_____

_____

Does the main character have at least two major problems in her life? Which offers the most potential for conflict?

_____

_____

_____

_____

_____

_____

How will the antagonist work against the main character? How will the antagonist stand in the main character's way and keep her from achieving her goal?

_____

_____

_____

_____

_____

_____

_____

Where will the story end?

_____

_____

_____

_____

_____

_____

What will the ideal reader expect of the story? How can you offer him the unexpected?

_____

_____

_____

_____

_____

_____

_____

_____

Additional notes:

_____

_____

_____

_____

_____

_____

Want to sketch something?

OUTLINING

Brief Instructions

This section is designed to help you come up with new ideas or develop the ones you already have. You can use the answers you wrote in the pre-writing section as a basis here and develop them into fuller settings, scenes, and characters.

The following outlining sections are divided into:

- World / Country / City
- Setting
- Scene
- Main Character Sketch
- Antagonist Sketch
- Major Character Sketch
- Minor Character Sketch

There are different amounts of these templates and sketches, which means that if you're planning a novel, you won't be able to outline your *entire* story in this workbook. However, you can **hop on over to my website and download more of these templates and sketches** if you need them. They are, of course, **free**.

You can find the templates and sketches on:

thewritingkylie.com/the-novel-planner-workbook-downloads

Now, let's get back to this workbook. I have provided you with a solid amount of these templates to start with. Here are a few tips on what to do:

- There is **1 template for the world / country / city** in which your story takes place. This template is meant to help you with the groundwork of the "bigger-picture" setting of the story.

- There are **6 setting templates** meant to help you outline the settings that are *most important and prominent* in your story. A story can have more or fewer settings, so, focus on the most important ones.

- There are **20 scene templates**. A novel will most likely have a lot more scenes then that, so, focus on *the major and important ones.*

- There is **1 main character sketch** meant for the character the story centers around. You may want to have more than one main character, if so, you can either download another template *or* use a template designed for a major character in this workbook.

- There is **1 antagonist sketch** meant for the major antagonist / antagonistic force of the story.

- There are **6 major character sketches** meant for those that have a *prominent role* in the story, either by supporting and helping the main character (like friends, mentors, etc.) or by creating conflict or opposing the main character in her everyday life (like minor antagonists, bullies, etc.).

- There are **6 minor character sketches** meant for those that *flesh out the world* but doesn't have a prominent role in the story.

Don't stay too long by sections if you don't know what to write. You can always go back later and write down your ideas as they come to you.

"By failing to prepare, you are preparing to fail."
— Benjamin Franklin

World / Country / City

Name: _____

Period / era: _____

The geographical location:

_____

_____

_____

_____

_____

_____

_____

The technological level and infrastructure:

_____

_____

_____

_____

_____

_____

The weather:

_____

_____

_____

_____

_____

Flora: Fauna:

_____   _____

_____   _____

_____   _____

_____   _____

_____   _____

_____   _____

_____   _____

_____   _____

_____   _____

_____   _____

_____   _____

Local authorities:

Laws:

_____

_____

_____

_____

_____

_____

_____

_____

_____

_____

_____

Local working possibilities:

_____

_____

_____

_____

_____

Local customs and traditions:

_____

_____

_____

_____

_____

_____

Local history:

_____

_____

_____

_____

_____

Additional notes:

_____

_____

_____

_____

Setting

Title: _____

Sight:

_____

_____

_____

_____

_____

_____

Smell:

_____

_____

_____

_____

_____

_____

Sound:

_____

_____

_____

_____

_____

_____

Taste:

Touch:

_____

_____

_____

_____

_____

_____

_____

_____

_____

_____

How the period / era affects the setting:

_____

_____

_____

_____

_____

Additional notes:

_____

_____

_____

_____

Setting

Title: _____

Sight:

_____

_____

_____

_____

_____

_____

_____

Smell:

_____

_____

_____

_____

_____

_____

Sound:

_____

_____

_____

_____

_____

_____

Taste:

Touch:

_____

_____

_____

_____

_____

How the period / era affects the setting:

_____

_____

_____

_____

_____

Additional notes:

_____

_____

_____

_____

Setting

Title: _____

Sight:

_____

_____

_____

_____

_____

_____

_____

Smell:

_____

_____

_____

_____

_____

_____

Sound:

_____

_____

_____

_____

_____

_____

Taste:

_____

_____

_____

_____

_____

Touch:

_____

_____

_____

_____

_____

How the period / era affects the setting:

_____

_____

_____

_____

_____

Additional notes:

_____

_____

_____

_____

Setting

Title: _____

Sight:

_____

_____

_____

_____

_____

_____

Smell:

_____

_____

_____

_____

_____

Sound:

_____

_____

_____

_____

_____

Taste:

Touch:

_____   _____

_____   _____

_____   _____

_____   _____

_____   _____

How the period / era affects the setting:

_____

_____

_____

_____

_____

Additional notes:

_____

_____

_____

_____

Setting

Title: _____

Sight:

_____

_____

_____

_____

_____

_____

_____

Smell:

_____   Sound:

_____   _____

_____   _____

_____   _____

_____   _____

_____   _____

_____   _____

Taste:

Touch:

_____

_____

_____

_____

_____

_____

_____

_____

_____

_____

_____

_____

How the period / era affects the setting:

_____

_____

_____

_____

_____

Additional notes:

_____

_____

_____

_____

_____

Setting

Title: _____

Sight:

_____

_____

_____

_____

_____

_____

Smell: Sound:

_____   _____

_____   _____

_____   _____

_____   _____

_____   _____

_____   _____

Taste:

Touch:

_____   _____

_____   _____

_____   _____

_____   _____

_____   _____

_____   _____

How the period / era affects the setting:

_____

_____

_____

_____

_____

_____

Additional notes:

_____

_____

_____

_____

_____

Scene

Title: _____

Date / timeline: _____

Setting:

_____

_____

_____

Description:

_____

_____

_____

_____

_____

_____

_____

_____

_____

_____

Scene

Title: _____

Date / timeline: _____

Setting:

_____

_____

_____

Description:

_____

_____

_____

_____

_____

_____

_____

_____

_____

_____

_____

Scene

Title:

Date / timeline:

_____

_____

Setting:

_____

_____

_____

Description:

_____

_____

_____

_____

_____

_____

_____

_____

_____

_____

_____

Scene

Title: _____   Date / timeline: _____

Setting:

_____

_____

_____

Description:

_____

_____

_____

_____

_____

_____

_____

_____

_____

Scene

Title: _____

Date / timeline: _____

Setting:

_____

_____

_____

Description:

_____

_____

_____

_____

_____

_____

_____

_____

_____

_____

Scene

Title:

Date / timeline:

_____

_____

Setting:

_____

_____

_____

Description:

_____

_____

_____

_____

_____

_____

_____

_____

_____

Scene

Title:

Date / timeline:

_____

_____

Setting:

_____

_____

_____

Description:

_____

_____

_____

_____

_____

_____

_____

_____

_____

_____

_____

Scene

Title: _____

Date / timeline: _____

Setting:

_____

_____

_____

Description:

_____

_____

_____

_____

_____

_____

_____

_____

_____

Scene

Title: _____

Date / timeline: _____

Setting:

_____

_____

_____

Description:

_____

_____

_____

_____

_____

_____

_____

_____

_____

_____

_____

Scene

Title:

Date / timeline:

_____

_____

Setting:

_____

_____

_____

Description:

_____

_____

_____

_____

_____

_____

_____

_____

_____

Scene

Title: _____

Date / timeline: _____

Setting:

_____

_____

_____

Description:

_____

_____

_____

_____

_____

_____

_____

_____

_____

_____

Scene

Title:

Date / timeline:

_____

_____

Setting:

_____

_____

_____

Description:

_____

_____

_____

_____

_____

_____

_____

_____

_____

_____

Scene

Title:

_____

Date / timeline:

_____

Setting:

_____

_____

_____

Description:

_____

_____

_____

_____

_____

_____

_____

_____

_____

_____

_____

Scene

Title: _____

Date / timeline: _____

Setting:

_____

_____

_____

Description:

_____

_____

_____

_____

_____

_____

_____

_____

_____

_____

_____

Scene

Title: _____

Date / timeline: _____

Setting:

_____

_____

_____

Description:

_____

_____

_____

_____

_____

_____

_____

_____

_____

_____

Scene

Title:

Date / timeline:

_____

_____

Setting:

_____

_____

_____

Description:

_____

_____

_____

_____

_____

_____

_____

_____

_____

_____

_____

Scene

Title:

Date / timeline:

_____

_____

Setting:

_____

_____

_____

Description:

_____

_____

_____

_____

_____

_____

_____

_____

_____

_____

Scene

Title:

Date / timeline:

_____

_____

Setting:

_____

_____

_____

Description:

_____

_____

_____

_____

_____

_____

_____

_____

_____

_____

_____

Scene

Title: _____

Date / timeline: _____

Setting:

_____

_____

_____

Description:

_____

_____

_____

_____

_____

_____

_____

_____

_____

Scene

Title: _____

Date / timeline: _____

Setting:

_____

_____

_____

Description:

_____

_____

_____

_____

_____

_____

_____

_____

_____

_____

Main Character Sketch

Name:

_____

Age:

_____

Physical description:

_____

_____

_____

_____

_____

Notable features:

_____

_____

_____

_____

_____

Backstory:

_____

_____

_____

_____

_____

What background information about her is essential for the reader to know in the opening of the story?

_____

_____

_____

_____

_____

Personality

Strengths:

_____

_____

_____

_____

_____

_____

_____

_____

Flaws:

_____

_____

_____

_____

_____

_____

_____

_____

Habits:

_____

_____

_____

_____

_____

Mannerisms:

_____

_____

_____

_____

_____

Story arc

Beginning: Middle: End:

_____   _____   _____

_____   _____   _____

_____   _____   _____

_____   _____   _____

_____   _____   _____

_____   _____   _____

_____   _____   _____

_____   _____   _____

_____   _____   _____

_____   _____   _____

_____   _____   _____

_____   _____   _____

Story goal: Motivation:

_____   _____

_____   _____

_____   _____

_____   _____

_____   _____

What does she stand to lose if she fails to achieve her goal?

_____

_____

_____

_____

_____

_____

_____

_____

_____

What does she stand to gain if she achieves her goal?

_____

_____

_____

_____

_____

_____

_____

_____

_____

The worst thing that can happen to the character:

_____

_____

_____

_____

How will her journey surprise the reader? How can you offer the reader the unexpected?

_____

_____

_____

_____

Antagonist Sketch

Name: Age:

_____   _____

Physical description: Notable features:

_____   _____

_____   _____

_____   _____

_____   _____

_____   _____

Backstory: What background information about
                                         her is essential for the reader to know
                                         in the opening of the story?

_____   _____

_____   _____

_____   _____

_____   _____

_____   _____

_____   _____

Personality

Strengths:

_____

_____

_____

_____

_____

_____

_____

_____

_____

Flaws:

_____

_____

_____

_____

_____

_____

_____

_____

_____

Habits:

_____

_____

_____

_____

_____

Mannerisms:

_____

_____

_____

_____

_____

Story arc

Beginning: Middle: End:

_____

_____

_____

_____

_____

_____

_____

_____

_____

_____

Story goal: Motivation:

_____

_____

_____

_____

_____

What does she stand to lose if she fails to achieve her goal?

_____

_____

_____

_____

_____

_____

_____

_____

_____

What does she stand to gain if she achieves her goal?

_____

_____

_____

_____

_____

_____

_____

_____

_____

The worst thing that can happen to the character:

_____

_____

_____

_____

How will her journey surprise the reader? How can you offer the reader the unexpected?

_____

_____

_____

_____

Major Character Sketch

Name:

Age:

_____

_____

Role

◯ Supportive Character

◯ Antagonistic Character / Force

Physical description:

Notable features:

_____

_____

_____

_____

_____

_____

_____

_____

Backstory:

What background information about her is essential for the reader to know right away?

_____

_____

_____

_____

_____

_____

_____

_____

Personality

Strengths:

_____

_____

_____

_____

_____

_____

_____

_____

Flaws:

_____

_____

_____

_____

_____

_____

_____

_____

Habits:

_____

_____

_____

_____

_____

_____

Mannerisms:

_____

_____

_____

_____

_____

_____

Story arc
Beginning: Middle: End:

_____   _____   _____

_____   _____   _____

_____   _____   _____

_____   _____   _____

_____   _____   _____

_____   _____   _____

_____   _____   _____

_____   _____   _____

_____   _____   _____

_____   _____   _____

_____   _____   _____

Story goal: Motivation:

_____   _____

_____   _____

_____   _____

_____   _____

_____   _____

_____   _____

The worst thing that can happen to the character:

How will her journey surprise the reader? How can you offer the reader the unexpected?

_____

_____

_____

_____

_____

_____

Additional notes:

_____

_____

_____

_____

_____

_____

_____

Major Character Sketch

Name:

Age:

_____

_____

Role

◯ Supportive Character

◯ Antagonistic Character / Force

Physical description:

Notable features:

_____

_____

_____

_____

_____

_____

_____

_____

Backstory:

What background information about her is essential for the reader to know right away?

_____

_____

_____

_____

_____

_____

_____

_____

Personality

Strengths:

_____

_____

_____

_____

_____

_____

_____

_____

Flaws:

_____

_____

_____

_____

_____

_____

_____

_____

Habits:

_____

_____

_____

_____

_____

Mannerisms:

_____

_____

_____

_____

_____

Story arc
Beginning: Middle: End:

_____   _____   _____

_____   _____   _____

_____   _____   _____

_____   _____   _____

_____   _____   _____

_____   _____   _____

_____   _____   _____

_____   _____   _____

_____   _____   _____

_____   _____   _____

_____   _____   _____

Story goal: Motivation:

_____   _____

_____   _____

_____   _____

_____   _____

_____   _____

The worst thing that can happen to the character:

How will her journey surprise the reader? How can you offer the reader the unexpected?

_____

_____

_____

_____

_____

_____

Additional notes:

_____

_____

_____

_____

_____

_____

_____

_____

Major Character Sketch

Name:

_____

Age:

_____

Role

O Supportive Character

O Antagonistic Character / Force

Physical description:

_____

_____

_____

_____

Notable features:

_____

_____

_____

_____

Backstory:

_____

_____

_____

_____

_____

What background information about her is essential for the reader to know right away?

_____

_____

_____

_____

_____

Personality

Strengths:

Flaws:

_____

_____

_____

_____

_____

_____

_____

_____

Habits:

Mannerisms:

_____

_____

_____

_____

_____

_____

_____

_____

Story arc

Beginning: Middle: End:

_____   _____   _____

_____   _____   _____

_____   _____   _____

_____   _____   _____

_____   _____   _____

_____   _____   _____

_____   _____   _____

_____   _____   _____

_____   _____   _____

_____   _____   _____

_____   _____   _____

Story goal: Motivation:

_____   _____

_____   _____

_____   _____

_____   _____

_____   _____

The worst thing that can happen to the character:

How will her journey surprise the reader? How can you offer the reader the unexpected?

_____

_____

_____

_____

_____

_____

_____

_____

_____

_____

_____

_____

_____

_____

Additional notes:

_____

_____

_____

_____

_____

_____

_____

_____

Major Character Sketch

Name:

_____

Age:

_____

Role

⭕ Supportive Character

⭕ Antagonistic Character / Force

Physical description:

_____

_____

_____

_____

Notable features:

_____

_____

_____

_____

Backstory:

What background information about her is essential for the reader to know right away?

_____

_____

_____

_____

_____

_____

_____

_____

_____

_____

Personality

Strengths:

_____

_____

_____

_____

_____

_____

_____

_____

Flaws:

_____

_____

_____

_____

_____

_____

_____

_____

Habits:

_____

_____

_____

_____

_____

Mannerisms:

_____

_____

_____

_____

_____

Story arc
Beginning: Middle: End:

_____   _____   _____

_____   _____   _____

_____   _____   _____

_____   _____   _____

_____   _____   _____

_____   _____   _____

_____   _____   _____

_____   _____   _____

_____   _____   _____

_____   _____   _____

_____   _____   _____

Story goal: Motivation:

_____   _____

_____   _____

_____   _____

_____   _____

_____   _____

The worst thing that can happen to the character:

How will her journey surprise the reader? How can you offer the reader the unexpected?

_____

_____

_____

_____

_____

_____

Additional notes:

_____

_____

_____

_____

_____

_____

_____

_____

Major Character Sketch

Name:

Age:

_____

_____

Role

O Supportive Character

O Antagonistic Character / Force

Physical description:

Notable features:

_____

_____

_____

_____

_____

_____

_____

_____

Backstory:

What background information about her is essential for the reader to know right away?

_____

_____

_____

_____

_____

_____

_____

_____

Personality

Strengths:

_____

_____

_____

_____

_____

_____

_____

Flaws:

_____

_____

_____

_____

_____

_____

_____

Habits:

_____

_____

_____

_____

_____

Mannerisms:

_____

_____

_____

_____

_____

Story arc
Beginning: Middle: End:

_____

_____

_____

_____

_____

_____

_____

_____

_____

_____

_____

Story goal: Motivation:

_____

_____

_____

_____

_____

_____

The worst thing that can happen to the character:

How will her journey surprise the reader? How can you offer the reader the unexpected?

_____

_____

_____

_____

_____

_____

Additional notes:

_____

_____

_____

_____

_____

_____

_____

_____

Major Character Sketch

Name: Age:

_____   _____

Role

◯ Supportive Character   ◯ Antagonistic Character / Force

Physical description: Notable features:

_____   _____

_____   _____

_____   _____

_____   _____

Backstory: What background information about her is essential for the reader to know right away?

_____   _____

_____   _____

_____   _____

_____   _____

Personality

Strengths:

_____

_____

_____

_____

_____

_____

_____

Flaws:

_____

_____

_____

_____

_____

_____

_____

Habits:

_____

_____

_____

_____

_____

Mannerisms:

_____

_____

_____

_____

_____

Story arc

Beginning: Middle: End:

_____   _____   _____

_____   _____   _____

_____   _____   _____

_____   _____   _____

_____   _____   _____

_____   _____   _____

_____   _____   _____

_____   _____   _____

_____   _____   _____

_____   _____   _____

_____   _____   _____

Story goal: Motivation:

_____   _____

_____   _____

_____   _____

_____   _____

_____   _____

The worst thing that can happen to the character:

How will her journey surprise the reader? How can you offer the reader the unexpected?

_____

_____

_____

_____

_____

_____

Additional notes:

_____

_____

_____

_____

_____

_____

_____

Minor Character Sketch

Name: _____

Age: _____

Physical description:

_____

_____

_____

_____

Notable features:

_____

_____

_____

_____

Backstory:

_____

_____

_____

_____

_____

_____

Strengths:

_____

Flaws:

_____

Habits:

_____

Mannerisms:

_____

Story arc

Beginning: Middle: End:

_____   _____   _____

_____   _____   _____

_____   _____   _____

_____   _____   _____

_____   _____   _____

_____   _____   _____

_____   _____   _____

_____   _____   _____

Story goal: Motivation:

_____   _____

_____   _____

_____   _____

_____   _____

Additional notes:

_____

_____

_____

_____

Minor Character Sketch

Name:

_____

Age:

_____

Physical description:

_____

_____

_____

_____

Notable features:

_____

_____

_____

_____

Backstory:

_____

_____

_____

_____

_____

Strengths:

_____

_____

Flaws:

_____

_____

Habits:

_____

_____

Mannerisms:

_____

_____

Story arc

Beginning: Middle: End:

————————————————   ————————————————   ————————————————

————————————————   ————————————————   ————————————————

————————————————   ————————————————   ————————————————

————————————————   ————————————————   ————————————————

————————————————   ————————————————   ————————————————

————————————————   ————————————————   ————————————————

————————————————   ————————————————   ————————————————

——————————   ——————————   ——————————

Story goal: Motivation:

————————————————————   ————————————————————

————————————————————   ————————————————————

————————————————————   ————————————————————

————————————————————   ————————————————————

Additional notes:

——

——

——

——

Minor Character Sketch

Name:

_____

Age:

_____

Physical description:

_____

_____

_____

_____

Notable features:

_____

_____

_____

_____

Backstory:

_____

_____

_____

_____

_____

_____

Strengths:

_____

_____

Flaws:

_____

_____

Habits:

_____

_____

Mannerisms:

_____

_____

Story arc

Beginning: Middle: End:

_____   _____   _____

_____   _____   _____

_____   _____   _____

_____   _____   _____

_____   _____   _____

_____   _____   _____

_____   _____   _____

_____   _____   _____

Story goal: Motivation:

_____   _____

_____   _____

_____   _____

_____   _____

Additional notes:

_____

_____

_____

_____

Minor Character Sketch

Name:

_____

Age:

_____

Physical description:

_____

_____

_____

_____

Notable features:

_____

_____

_____

_____

Backstory:

_____

_____

_____

_____

_____

_____

Strengths:

_____

_____

Flaws:

_____

_____

Habits:

_____

_____

Mannerisms:

_____

_____

Story arc

Beginning: Middle: End:

_____   _____   _____

_____   _____   _____

_____   _____   _____

_____   _____   _____

_____   _____   _____

_____   _____   _____

_____   _____   _____

Story goal: Motivation:

_____   _____

_____   _____

_____   _____

_____   _____

Additional notes:

_____

_____

_____

_____

Minor Character Sketch

Name:

_____

Age:

_____

Physical description:

_____

_____

_____

_____

Notable features:

_____

_____

_____

_____

Backstory:

_____

_____

_____

_____

_____

_____

Strengths:

_____

_____

Flaws:

_____

Habits:

_____

Mannerisms:

_____

_____

Story arc

Beginning: Middle: End:

_____   _____   _____

_____   _____   _____

_____   _____   _____

_____   _____   _____

_____   _____   _____

_____   _____   _____

_____   _____   _____

_____   _____   _____

Story goal: Motivation:

_____   _____

_____   _____

_____   _____

_____   _____

Additional notes:

_____

_____

_____

_____

Minor Character Sketch

Name: _____

Age: _____

Physical description:

_____

_____

_____

_____

Notable features:

_____

_____

_____

_____

Backstory:

_____

_____

_____

_____

_____

Strengths:

_____

Flaws:

_____

Habits:

_____

Mannerisms:

_____

Story arc

Beginning: Middle: End:

_____   _____   _____

_____   _____   _____

_____   _____   _____

_____   _____   _____

_____   _____   _____

_____   _____   _____

_____   _____   _____

_____   _____   _____

Story goal: Motivation:

_____   _____

_____   _____

_____   _____

_____   _____

Additional notes:

_____

_____

_____

_____

Want to sketch something?

STORY
STRUCTURE

Seven Point Story Structure Explanation

Hook: The main character's starting point. This is the opposite of the **Resolution**.

Plot Turn 1: The event that sets the story in motion and moves from the beginning to the **Midpoint**. Introduce the conflict. The main character's world changes—basically when the main character sets out on her journey.

Pinch Point 1: Apply pressure. This is often used to introduce the antagonist / antagonistic force.

Midpoint: The main character moves from reaction to action. She determines she must do something to stop the antagonist.

Pinch Point 2: Apply more pressure. The story takes the ultimate dive. The main character is at her darkest moment and seems to have lost everything.

Plot Turn 2: The story moves from **Midpoint** to the **Resolution**. The main character gets or realizes she has the final piece of information to achieve what she set out to do in the **Midpoint**.

Resolution: The climax. Everything in the story leads to this moment. Here, the main character achieves what she set out to do (or fails to do so, depending on your story).

The easiest and most effective order in which to write down the events:

1. Resolution
2. Hook
3. Midpoint
4. Plot turn 1
5. Plot turn 2
6. Pinch point 1
7. Pinch point 2.

Seven Point Story Structure

Hook:

_____

_____

Plot Turn 1:

_____

_____

_____

_____

Pinch Point 1:

_____

_____

Midpoint:

_____

_____

_____

_____

Pinch Point 2:

_____

_____

Plot Turn 2:

_____

_____

_____

_____

Resolution:

_____

_____

_____

_____

_____

Additional notes:

_____

_____

_____

Want to sketch something?

PROJECT OVERVIEW

Project Overview

Title of project:

_____

Genre:

_____

Length: Novel   Novella   Short Story

Estimated word count: _____

Setting:

_____

_____

_____

_____

Themes:

_____

_____

_____

_____

Summary of project:

_____

_____

_____

_____

_____

_____

_____

Character list
Main Character: Antagonist:

_____   _____

_____   _____

_____   _____

Other major characters: Minor characters:

_____   _____

_____   _____

_____   _____

_____   _____

_____   _____

_____   _____

Additional notes:

_____

_____

_____

_____

_____

_____

_____

_____

Want to sketch something?

RESEARCH LIST

○ _____
○ _____
○ _____
○ _____
○ _____
○ _____
○ _____
○ _____
○ _____
○ _____
○ _____
○ _____
○ _____
○ _____
○ _____
○ _____
○ _____
○ _____
○ _____
○ _____
○ _____

○ _____
○ _____
○ _____
○ _____
○ _____
○ _____
○ _____
○ _____
○ _____
○ _____
○ _____
○ _____
○ _____
○ _____
○ _____
○ _____
○ _____
○ _____
○ _____
○ _____
○ _____

○ _____
○ _____
○ _____
○ _____
○ _____
○ _____
○ _____
○ _____
○ _____
○ _____
○ _____
○ _____
○ _____
○ _____
○ _____
○ _____
○ _____
○ _____
○ _____
○ _____
○ _____
○ _____

○ _____
○ _____
○ _____
○ _____
○ _____
○ _____
○ _____
○ _____
○ _____
○ _____
○ _____
○ _____
○ _____
○ _____
○ _____
○ _____
○ _____
○ _____
○ _____
○ _____
○ _____
○ _____

Want to sketch something?

The Ultimate Story Checklist

Characters

O Does the story have a clear main character?

O Does the story have a clear antagonist (either a physical antagonist or an antagonistic force)?

O Does the story have a supporting cast (other major characters that help the main character)?

O Does the story have minor antagonists that add obstacles and conflicts to the main character's life?

O Does the main character have a goal that drives her forward?

O Does the main character have a clear arc demonstrating her change and/or growth?

O How does the supporting cast contribute to the main character's journey? They are not major characters (or particularly important) if they don't support and help the main character on her journey. Evaluate these characters and decide whether to keep them in the story.

O Are the minor characters explored in too much detail and therefore take away focus from the important events of the story? If so, either make a minor character a major one that is more involved in the story — and have her contribute to the main character's journey — or take focus away from the minor character to center the attention on the important events of the story.

O Are any of the characters clichéd or stereotypical? How can you change this?

O Does any of the characters play a surprising role at the end? This is not necessary, but it will add an interesting twist to the ending.

O Have you given the reader enough information about the background of the characters (family, education, important events, etc.) so that the reader understand them?

O How have you given the information about the characters to the reader? Have you sprinkled it throughout the novel or offered it in bigger info-dumping chunks? Aim for the sprinkled version.

○ Do the characters behave in ways that are consistent with their backgrounds?

Additional notes:

_____

_____

_____

_____

_____

_____

_____

_____

_____

_____

_____

_____

_____

_____

Setting

○ Does the story have a major setting where most of the story's events take place?

○ Does the story have any minor settings (the main character's workplace, a friend's home, etc.)?

○ Do the settings contribute something to the story, like enhancing the plot or adding conflict to the story?

○ Do you introduce the settings with too much description all in one go (info-dumping)?

○ Have you paid enough attention to the smells and sounds in the settings? Smell and sound are the most important senses to create an atmosphere.

○ Are the settings memorable and do they fit the mood of your story?

Additional notes:

_____

_____

_____

_____

_____

_____

_____

_____

_____

Plot

O Does the first part of the plot set up the problem (main conflict) and create tension?

O Does the middle part of the plot deepen the problem and challenge the main character?

O Does the final part of the plot provide a resolution, and if so, does it affect the main character in an essential way? Make sure the whole journey to this point has affected the main character in a big way (good or bad).

O Do the subplots advance the plot? Are they eventually resolved? If not, make sure they both advance the plot and are resolved. Tie up all loose ends. (However, if you're writing a series where the subplot in one book will be resolved in the beginning of the next book — or even develop into the main plot of the next book — you may be excused for leaving this subplot unresolved.)

O Are there any scenes that do not serve the plot? You need to consider cutting them even if they are written well.

O Are there any plot holes you need to fix?

O Do you rush through the big plot points / main events? Consider slowing down when writing these events so they won't take the form of a summary.

O What big plot points / main events can you go back and foreshadow earlier in the story to craft a cohesive and well-rounded story?

O Is it easy to follow the passage of time through the story?

Additional notes:

_____

_____

_____

Point-of-View

○ Which point-of-view are you using (first person, third person, omniscient, etc.)? What are the benefits of this point-of-view? Are there any drawbacks?

○ Do you have one or several point-of-view characters? Would the story be better if you stuck with a single point-of-view character? Would the story be better if you added another point-of-view character?

○ Would the story be better if you changed the point-of-view (first person, third person, omniscient, etc.) for the entire story?

○ Is the point-of-view consistent throughout the story? Do you head-hop? If so, revise to avoid head-hopping.

○ Is the voice right and consistent for the point-of-view character?

○ Does the point-of-view character know or see things she couldn't realistically know or see?

Additional notes:

_____

_____

_____

_____

_____

_____

_____

_____

Dialogue

○ Does the speech of each character fit their personality and background?

○ Are you using dialogue as info-dumps?

○ Does the dialogue sound natural or stilted and monotone? Would the dialogue sound more realistic if you used more contractions and mixed up the length of the sentences? Would it feel more alive if you incorporated body language where words are superfluous? Body language is vital to show what a character is feeling or what kind of state-of-mind she is in without having her say it out loud.

○ Do you use commonplace dialogue (hello, goodbye, yes, no, etc.), and if so, does it add to the dialogue? Can the dialogue do without them?

○ Have you filled the dialogue with unnecessary explanation (like: "You son of a bitch!" he *yelled angrily*)?

○ How many -ly adverbs (angrily, happily, sadly, etc.) have you used? Are there too many?

Additional notes:

_____

_____

_____

_____

_____

_____

_____

Notes:

Notes:

THANK YOU!

I hope The Novel Planner Workbook has been valuable to you, and that you've enjoyed using it.

If you have any suggestions on how I can improve this workbook, don't hesitate to get in touch.

Also, I would love it if you send me a photo of you using the planner.

Contact

Website: TheWritingKylie.com
Email: kylie@thewritingkylie.com
Facebook: @TheWritingKylie
Twitter: @kylieday0

56461377R00086

Made in the USA
San Bernardino, CA
11 November 2017